This Book Belongs to

_____

Thank you

To ensure that you have the best experience using this coloring book and to prevent bleeding, although the illustrations are on one-side, we recommend coloring using pencils.

If you are going to use any kind of ink that may cause bleeding through out the papers, we recommend tearing out the coloring pages or using a buffer page. (you can find blank buffer pages at the end of the book.)

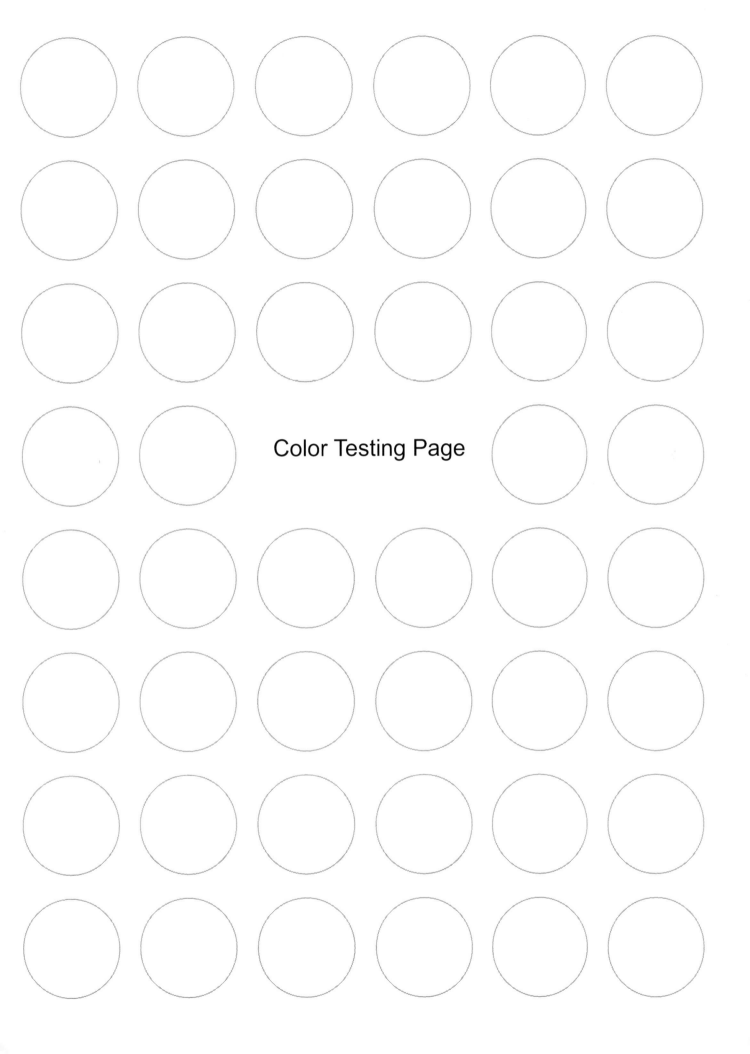

Color Testing Page

This page is intentionally left blank to avoid color bleeding.

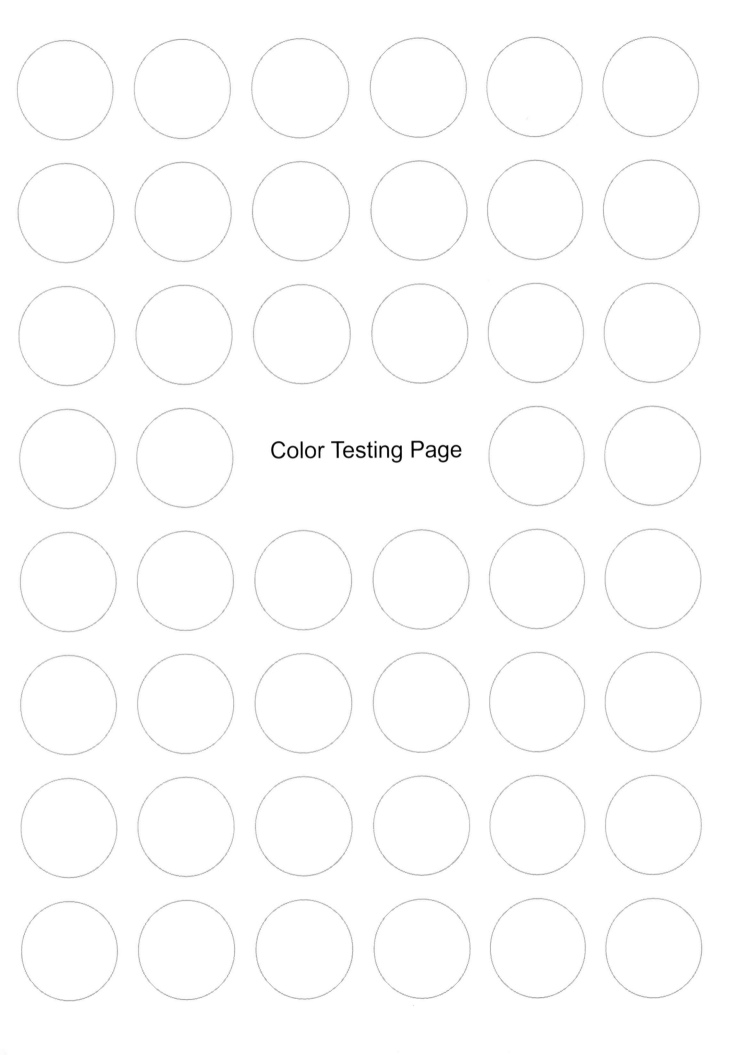

Color Testing Page

This page is intentionally left blank to avoid color bleeding.

This page is intentionally left blank to avoid color bleeding.

This page is intentionally left blank to avoid color bleeding.

This page is intentionally left blank to avoid color bleeding.

This page is intentionally left blank to avoid color bleeding.

This page is intentionally left blank to avoid color bleeding.

This page is intentionally left blank to avoid color bleeding.

This page is intentionally left blank to avoid color bleeding.

This page is intentionally left blank to avoid color bleeding.

This page is intentionally left blank to avoid color bleeding.

This page is intentionally left blank to avoid color bleeding.

This page is intentionally left blank to avoid color bleeding.

This page is intentionally left blank to avoid color bleeding.

This page is intentionally left blank to avoid color bleeding.

This page is intentionally left blank to avoid color bleeding.

This page is intentionally left blank to avoid color bleeding.

This page is intentionally left blank to avoid color bleeding.

This page is intentionally left blank to avoid color bleeding.

This page is intentionally left blank to avoid color bleeding.

This page is intentionally left blank to avoid color bleeding.

This page is intentionally left blank to avoid color bleeding.

This page is intentionally left blank to avoid color bleeding.

This page is intentionally left blank to avoid color bleeding.

This page is intentionally left blank to avoid color bleeding.

This page is intentionally left blank to avoid color bleeding.

This page is intentionally left blank to avoid color bleeding.

This page is intentionally left blank to avoid color bleeding.

This page is intentionally left blank to avoid color bleeding.

This page is intentionally left blank to avoid color bleeding.

This page is intentionally left blank to avoid color bleeding.

This page is intentionally left blank to avoid color bleeding.

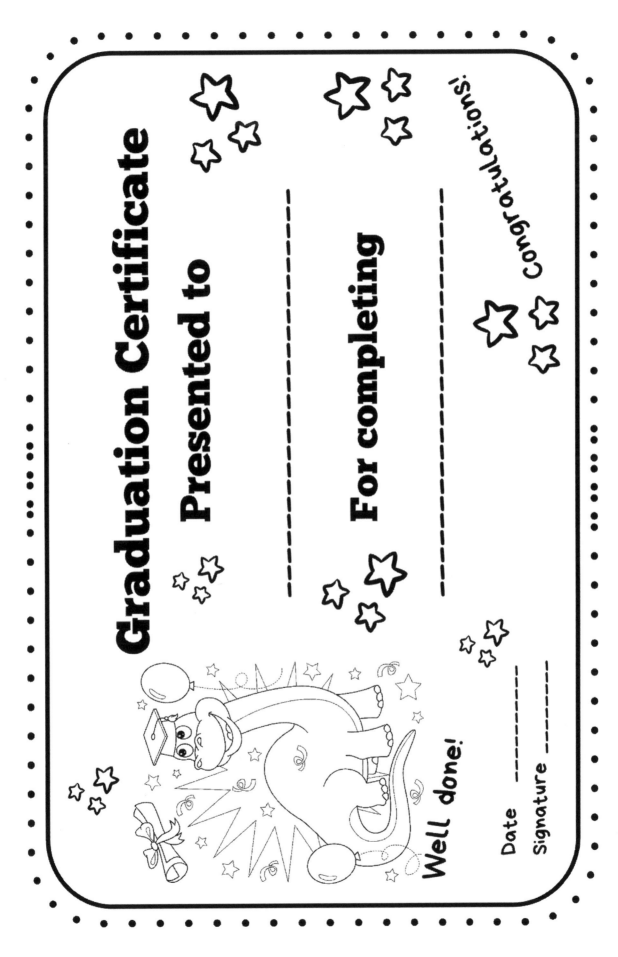

Graduation Certificate

Presented to

_ _ _ _ _ _ _ _ _ _

For completing

_ _ _ _ _ _ _ _ _ _

Congratulations!

Well done!

Date _ _ _ _ _ _

Signature _ _ _ _ _ _

Buffer paper

Please cut and use between pages when you color
with any ink that may cause bleeding.

This Page is Intentionally Left Blank.

Buffer paper

Please cut and use between pages when you color
with any ink that may cause bleeding.

This Page is Intentionally Left Blank.

Made in the USA
Monee, IL
04 June 2022